THE WORDS THAT SAVED ME

PowERFUL AFFIRMATIONS,
To REPROGRAM YOUR BRAIN & CHANGE
YOUR LIFE.

By: ASHTON ASHCROFT

Preface

I didn't write this book to impress anyone. I wrote it to make changing your life seem more accessible & less like a language you need permission to speak.

This is not an overly complicated guide. I kept it simple on purpose. Each affirmation is specific to a need you may have in your life.

Affirmations are not merely wishful thinking, They are a conscious reprogramming of ones own brain & higher self.

Most of us have gone through life on auto-pilot, allowing life to break us down & strip away the magic we once believed in.

I centered the text & left margins wide on both sides so you can scribe your own meanings, stories & experiences as you go.

My hope is that this book becomes a conversation between you & your higher self.

Listen to them.

Then write back.

Why This Book Exists

I'VE LIVED THROUGH THINGS THAT TORE HOLES IN THE STORY I
THOUGHT MY LIFE WOULD BE. GRIEF THAT NEVER LEFT.

LOVE THAT HURT. A BODY MARKED BY BOTH SURVIVAL &
STIGMA. SILENCE THAT NEARLY SWALLOWED ME.

THERE WERE TIMES I DIDN'T HAVE WORDS FOR WHAT I FELT.

AFFIRMATIONS HELPED GROUND ME IN THE MOMENT, MADE ME
FEEL SAFE & REALIZE, I AM PART OF THIS WORLD & NOT OF IT.

THEY HELPED ME MAKE MEANING OUT OF MOMENTS THAT FELT
SENSELESS, GAVE SHAPE TO THE CHAOS. SOMETIMES, THEY
JUST GAVE ME PERMISSION TO FEEL.

THIS BOOK ISN'T ABOUT OTHER THAN RECLAIMING YOUR POWER. I
WROTE IT AS SOMEONE WHO KNOWS WHAT IT'S LIKE TO SEARCH
FOR CLARITY IN THE DARK.

YOU'LL FIND STRUCTURE HERE, BUT ALSO ROOM TO GROW

IF YOU'VE EVER FELT LIKE YOUR STORY DIDN'T MAKE SENSE, OR
LIKE NO ONE GAVE YOU THE TOOLS TO TELL IT, LET THIS BE A
BEGINNING. A MIRROR. A MOMENT OF STILLNESS.

A WAY THROUGH.

DEDICATED TO YOU

FOR THE ONES WHO SURVIVED WHAT SHOULD HAVE BROKEN THEM.

FOR THE QUIET HEALERS, THE MISFITS, THE FEELERS, THE FORGOTTEN.

FOR EVERY TIME YOU PICKED UP THE PIECES & CALLED IT A RITUAL.

FOR THE VERSION OF ME THAT DIDN'T THINK THEY'D MAKE IT THIS FAR.

THIS IS FOR YOU.

THIS IS FOR US.

I AM BECAUSE I FEEL, I DO BECAUSE I LOVE.

I SPEAK INTO EXISTENCE, SO THAT I MAY SEE THE WORLD UNFOLD BEFORE ME.

I AM THAT I FEEL & I FEEL THAT I AM.

SO THAT I KNOW, THAT I AM.

How To Use This Book

This book isn't meant to be read cover to cover.

It's meant to be returned to, flipped open when you need insight, affirmation, or a different way to see something.

Use it like a mirror, a journal companion, or a study guide.

Each page has space around it for a reason.

Read these affirmations & create your own. Embrace what your mind, body & soul is telling you in each moment.

Let your intuition fill in the blanks.

Let this book grow with you.

When the meanings & moments don't make sense, sit with them anyway.

You're not wrong.

You're just in your own story & that's the only one that matters here.

Think before you speak

In each section of this book, we'll focus on a different type of affirmations. Each carries a unique vibration & speaks to a different layer of your becoming. To deepen the work, I've included a simple ritual for each category.

These are not for show. They're small, sacred acts that help anchor the affirmations into your body, your breath, & your everyday life.

Understand this: real change is not always soft. Reprogramming your mind means reordering your reality. People you once called friends may fall away. What used to matter may suddenly feel hollow. Your perspective may stretch beyond what you thought possible.

That's not a sign of failure it's a sign of alignment.

Don't speak these affirmations lightly. Let them settle in your chest before you ever open your mouth.

Think of your life like a still, serene body of water. Every thought you have is a quiet breeze, brushing across the surface, sending tiny ripples outward.

When you speak an affirmation, you're skipping a pebble across that water. It moves. It echoes. It returns.

But when you believe it, when you speak it with clarity & intention, it's like hurling a boulder straight into the center.

The waves don't stop at you. They reach the shore. They bounce back. They shift everything.

THIS BOOK IS NOT ABOUT FEELING GOOD FOR A MOMENT.

IT'S ABOUT AWAKENING THE VOICE THAT ALREADY LIVES INSIDE YOU THE ONE THAT REMEMBERS WHO YOU ARE & WHO YOU CAME HERE TO BECOME.

SPEAK WITH CARE.

SPEAK WITH POWER.

THEN WATCH WHAT CHANGES.

Self-Worth & Identity

Spell: The Mirror Claiming Ritual

Stand before a mirror, preferably naked or in simple clothes.

Light a white candle.

Look into your own eyes & repeat: "I see myself. I claim myself. I love myself as I am."

Say 3 affirmations aloud.

Anoint your chest with oil or water, saying: "I return to me."

Blow out the candle & thank your reflection.

Self-Worth & Identity

I am enough, exactly as I am.

I am whole, I am healing, I am free.

My value is not up for debate.

I deserve peace, not just survival.

I don't chase love; I embody it.

I am not my past.

I carry wisdom in every scar.

I forgive myself & start again.

I am safe in my own body.

I release shame. It doesn't belong to me.

I honor my own pace.

I get to define my life.

I am not too much. I am just right.

My truth is sacred.

I speak my needs without apology.

I am not broken. I am becoming.

I am a miracle in motion.

I breathe life into every room I enter.

I trust myself completely.

I belong here, now & always.

I am allowed to take up space.

I am valid in every version of me.

I choose to define myself.

My story deserves to be heard.

I do not need to shrink to fit in.

I am not behind; I am becoming.

My presence is powerful.

I belong to myself first.

I am allowed to evolve.

My identity is sacred.

Courage & Resilience
Spell: The Fire Bowl Burn & Rebuild Ritual

Write what you're afraid of or tired of carrying on a scrap of paper.

Burn it safely in a bowl or fire-safe container.

As the ashes cool, whisper: "I am not my fear. I am the flame that survives it."

Trace a symbol (like a rising sun, phoenix, or mountain) over your heart with your finger.

Say a courage affirmation out loud, like: "I face it all & keep rising."

Courage & Resilience

I rise every time I fall.

I face fear & move forward anyway.

I bend, but I do not break.

Every challenge grows me stronger.

I am unshakable.

I've overcome before, I will again.

I trust my resilience.

I meet difficulty with clarity & power.

I'm not here to shrink, I expand.

I am the storm & the calm inside it.

I keep going when others stop.

My scars are maps of survival.

I am brave enough to start over.

I DO HARD THINGS WITH GRACE.

I AM GROUNDED & IMMOVABLE.

I HAVE SURVIVED MY HARDEST DAYS.

I LEAD MYSELF WITH INTEGRITY.

I CLAIM MY SPACE WITHOUT FEAR.

I RELEASE THE NEED FOR APPROVAL.

I MAKE POWERFUL CHOICES.

Abundance & Wealth

Spell: The Salt & Cinnamon Sweep Ritual

Mix a handful of salt with a sprinkle of cinnamon in your palm.

Stand at the entrance of your home.

Blow the mix into the house while saying: "Wealth flows in & stays. My space welcomes abundance."

Say 3 wealth-focused affirmations.

Clean your floors after to seal the spell with order.

Abundance & Wealth

I attract wealth with ease.

Money flows to me consistently.

I am a magnet for opportunities.

I create income doing what I love.

My mind is wired for abundance.

I deserve to be well paid.

I release scarcity, I welcome overflow.

I trust my financial instincts.

Wealth supports my purpose.

I receive with gratitude & grace.

I break all limits around money.

My success helps others rise.

I am building generational wealth.

Every dollar I spend returns multiplied.

I manage money with confidence.

I make wealthy decisions daily.

My work is valuable & in demand.

I am open to unexpected blessings.

I have more than enough.

I trust life to meet my needs.

I am worthy of more than survival.

I trust in divine timing & flow.

I open to receive.

I welcome the unknown with gratitude.

I am aligned with wealth.

My prosperity uplifts others.

I am supported in every season.

I TRUST THERE IS ALWAYS MORE ON THE WAY.

I RECEIVE WITHOUT FEAR OR SHAME.

MY ABUNDANCE IS INEVITABLE.

Healing & Transformation

Spell: The Water Bowl Release Ritual

Fill a bowl with water.

Whisper into it: all the pain, guilt, shame, or grief you're ready to release.

Say: "I pour it out. I don't carry this anymore."

Take the bowl outside or to a sink & pour the water away slowly.

As it drains, say: "I heal, I grow, I return."

Healing &
Transformation

I release all that no longer serves me.

My healing is already underway.

I trust my body to heal.

My spirit is resilient & wise.

Every breath is a fresh beginning.

I allow myself to rest & receive.

I reclaim my power from trauma.

I choose softness without weakness.

I heal from the inside out.

I let go of the past & return to presence.

I rewrite the story of my life.

I treat myself with compassion.

I AM ALLOWED TO FEEL DEEPLY & STILL BE SAFE.

I HOLD SPACE FOR MY INNER CHILD.

MY NERVOUS SYSTEM IS RESETTING TO PEACE.

I CHOOSE JOY EVEN WHEN IT'S HARD.

I NOURISH EVERY PART OF ME.

I TRUST THE TIMING OF MY JOURNEY.

I EMBODY RENEWAL.

MY PAIN DOES NOT DEFINE ME.

I FORGIVE MYSELF FOR NOT KNOWING THEN.

I RELEASE OLD RESENTMENT.

I DO NOT CARRY WHAT IS NOT MINE.

I CUT CORDS WITH GRACE.

I FREE MYSELF FROM THE PAST.

I CHOOSE PEACE OVER ANGER.

I LET GO FOR MY OWN FREEDOM.

I FORGIVE OTHERS TO FREE MYSELF.

I MAKE SPACE FOR NEW ENERGY.

I CLEANSE MY SPIRIT WITH TRUTH.

Spiritual Power

Spell: The Smoke & Breath Alignment Ritual

Light incense or burn herbs like rosemary, mugwort, or frankincense.

Stand or sit in silence.

As the smoke rises, say: "I rise with spirit. I am guided."

Inhale deeply. On each exhale, say a spiritual affirmation like "I am aligned" or "I am protected."

End with gratitude: "Thank you to the unseen."

Spiritual Power

I walk in divine alignment.

I am guided by a higher purpose.

Spirit moves through me in every moment.

I am connected to everything.

My intuition is clear & accurate.

I am a vessel for truth & healing.

I am surrounded by unseen support.

I release control & surrender to flow.

I trust the signs I receive.

I call in what is meant for me.

I protect my energy with intention.

I am grounded & expanded at once.

The universe is working for my highest good.

I speak blessings into existence.

I honor my ancestors through my becoming.

My life is sacred.

I am a bridge between worlds.

I co-create with the divine.

I am open to magic.

I am light, even in the dark.

I walk in divine rhythm.

I am one with the universe.

I listen when spirit speaks.

I am connected to something greater.

I trust what I feel even when I can't explain it.

My soul always knows the way.

I am protected in every realm.

My ancestors walk beside me.

I honor the unseen.

I am light embodied.

Love & Relationships

Spell: The Rose Quartz & Whispered Names Ritual

Hold a rose quartz crystal or any object charged with loving energy.

Say your name out loud. Then say the names of people you love or want love with.

For each, whisper: "May love move freely between us, in truth, in peace, in joy."

Say: "I am love. I receive love. I give love."

Sleep with the crystal under your pillow.

Love & Relationships

I attract love that sees me fully.

I am worthy of deep, lasting connection.

I set boundaries that honor my soul.

I give & receive love freely.

I choose partners who choose me.

I am love in human form.

I am safe to open my heart.

I communicate with honesty & clarity.

I grow with those I love.

I am not afraid to be fully seen.

I do not beg for love, I embody it.

My presence is enough.

I am a mirror of sacred intimacy.

I RELEASE TOXIC DYNAMICS.

I CALL IN ALIGNED RELATIONSHIPS.

I KNOW HOW TO LOVE WITHOUT LOSING MYSELF.

I TRUST WHO I AM BECOMING IN LOVE.

I LET GO OF THOSE NOT MEANT FOR ME.

I GIVE LOVE WITHOUT FEAR OF ABANDONMENT.

I AM SURROUNDED BY SOUL FAMILY.

I LOVE WITH DEPTH & PRESENCE.

I DESERVE RELATIONSHIPS ROOTED IN TRUTH.

I ATTRACT THOSE WHO SEE & HONOR ME.

I EXPRESS LOVE WITHOUT FEAR.

I AM NOT HARD TO LOVE.

I CALL IN LOVE THAT IS NOURISHING.

I SPEAK LOVE FLUENTLY.

I DESERVE EASE IN CONNECTION.

I CREATE INTIMACY THROUGH HONESTY.

I LOVE FROM A FULL CUP.

CREATIVITY & PURPOSE

SPELL: THE INK & INTUITION WRITING RITUAL

LIGHT A CANDLE & TAKE A BLANK SHEET OF PAPER.

WITHOUT PLANNING, WRITE: "WHAT WANTS TO COME THROUGH ME TODAY?"

FREE WRITE OR DRAW FOR 5–10 MINUTES. NO RULES.

WHEN DONE, SAY: "I TRUST WHAT FLOWS. I HONOR THE VOICE WITHIN."

KEEP THE PAPER ON YOUR ALTAR OR BURN IT TO RELEASE THE ENERGY INTO THE WORLD.

CREATIVITY & PURPOSE

I AM HERE FOR A REASON.

MY VOICE MATTERS.

I CREATE FROM MY SOUL.

I GIVE LIFE TO IDEAS THAT INSPIRE.

MY CREATIVITY IS BOUNDLESS.

I TRUST THE PROCESS, NOT JUST THE RESULT.

I FOLLOW MY CURIOSITY WHEREVER IT LEADS.

I MAKE BEAUTY OUT OF CHAOS.

I AM ALWAYS EVOLVING.

MY WORK IS AN OFFERING TO THE WORLD.

I AM HERE TO DO MEANINGFUL THINGS.

I BIRTH NEW VISIONS WITH CONFIDENCE.

I EXPRESS MYSELF WITHOUT FEAR.

I trust my calling, even when it's quiet.

I allow creativity to flow through me.

I am an artist of my own life.

I act boldly on inspiration.

I release perfection & choose progress.

I am capable of extraordinary ideas.

I take action even when it's messy.

I walk my path with clarity.

I trust the unfolding of my journey.

My purpose is within me, not outside me.

I honor the work I am called to do.

I don't need permission to begin.

I create meaning through action.

My path is unique & necessary.

I ALIGN WITH WHAT SETS MY SOUL ON FIRE.

I MOVE WITH SACRED INTENTION.

I ALREADY AM WHAT I AM BECOMING.

I AM A VESSEL FOR CREATIVITY.

I AM NOT AFRAID TO BE SEEN.

I EXPRESS MYSELF FREELY & BOLDLY.

I AM CONSTANTLY CREATING BEAUTY.

I SHARE MY TRUTH WITHOUT FEAR.

I FOLLOW WHAT INSPIRES ME.

I TRUST THE CREATIVE PROCESS.

I HONOR MY UNIQUE VOICE.

Daily Power & Presence

Spell: The Grounding Touch Ritual

Place both hands on the earth, your belly, or the floor, whatever feels grounding.

Say: "I am here. I am now. I am ready."

Stand, stretch & speak a simple power affirmation out loud: "I claim this day. It is mine to shape."

Drink a glass of water with intention.

Daily Power & Presence

I start this day with purpose.

I claim the energy I want to feel.

I focus only on what I can control.

I release distractions & return to center.

I choose how I respond to life.

I listen before I react.

I am not behind. I'm exactly where I need to be.

I own my morning, I own my life.

I move with calm confidence.

I am present & powerful.

I lead my life with intention.

I honor my needs each day.

I create routines that nourish me.

I WAKE WITH GRATITUDE.

I REST WITHOUT GUILT.

I AM IN COMMAND OF MY FOCUS.

I BUILD MOMENTUM DAILY.

I RELEASE THE NEED TO DO IT ALL.

I SHOW UP EVEN WHEN I FEEL UNSURE.

I START SMALL & STAY CONSISTENT.

MY BODY IS MY HOME & I HONOR IT.

I RELEASE SHAME & CHOOSE REVERENCE.

I LISTEN TO WHAT MY BODY ASKS FOR.

I CELEBRATE WHAT MY BODY HAS CARRIED.

I AM ALLOWED TO REST.

I MOVE TO FEEL ALIVE, NOT TO PUNISH MYSELF.

I SPEAK LOVINGLY TO MY REFLECTION.

I TREAT MYSELF WITH TENDERNESS.

My body holds ancient wisdom.

I thank my body every day.

I am allowed to slow down.

My peace is a sacred priority.

I let go of urgency.

I create calm with every breath.

I release chaos & invite stillness.

I am a sanctuary.

I return to my center with ease.

I breathe in peace.

I choose presence over pressure.

I rest in the now.

Radical Self-Love

Spell: The Oil Anointing Ritual

Play a song that makes you feel powerful or beautiful.

Rub oil (olive, coconut, etc.) on your chest, belly, thighs, anywhere you carry shame.

For each touch, say: "This part of me is sacred. I love this."

Move your body slowly. Dance if it feels right.

Say: "I am the home I've been looking for."

Radical Self-Love

I speak to myself with kindness.

I cherish the person I'm becoming.

I choose softness over judgment.

I celebrate myself fully.

I am worthy of my own devotion.

I listen to my body's wisdom.

I respect my own limits.

I am allowed to take up space.

I honor my reflection.

I fall in love with myself a little more every day.

I prioritize myself without guilt.

I give myself permission to rest.

I don't compete, I align.

I EMBRACE ALL MY QUIRKS & GIFTS.

I LET GO OF WHAT OTHERS THINK.

I CHOOSE AUTHENTICITY OVER APPROVAL.

I NOURISH MYSELF IN EVERY WAY.

I DESERVE TENDERNESS.

I BLOOM IN MY OWN SEASON.

I AM MY OWN GREATEST LOVE STORY.

Rebirth, Destiny & Renewal

Spell: The Dirt & Candle Choice Ritual

Light a black or white candle.

Take a pinch of dirt, ash, or coffee grounds in one hand (representing the past).

Say: "I have walked through it. I'm still here."

Open your other hand & whisper: "Now I choose."

Blow the dirt into the wind or sprinkle it outside.

Say: "I walk into my life with open eyes."

Rebirth, Destiny & Renewal

I am not who I was yesterday.

I rise like the sun, daily.

I walk forward with purpose.

I call back every piece of myself.

I am the author of my life.

I close old chapters with peace.

I say yes to my becoming.

I walk in new timelines now.

I don't repeat cycles, I break them.

I am my ancestors' wildest dream.

I honor the fire inside me.

I plant new seeds with intention.

I LIVE ON PURPOSE.

I TRUST THE UNFOLDING.

I CHOOSE DESTINY OVER DOUBT.

I AM CONSTANTLY REBORN.

I EMBODY DIVINE TIMING.

I SHED WHAT NO LONGER FITS.

I WALK TOWARD THE FUTURE WITH OPEN ARMS.

I AM UNSTOPPABLE.

I AM NOT AFRAID TO BEGIN AGAIN.

I SHED WHAT NO LONGER FITS.

I RISE FROM ENDINGS WITH NEW EYES.

I AM THE PHOENIX & THE FLAME.

I MAKE PEACE WITH THE PAST.

I CLOSE OLD DOORS WITHOUT REGRET.

I RETURN TO MYSELF, OVER & OVER.

I EVOLVE UNAPOLOGETICALLY.

I AM IN CONSTANT TRANSFORMATION.

I TRUST WHAT'S EMERGING IN ME.

Confidence & Power

Spell: The Salt Step Ritual

Sprinkle a small line of salt before your doorway.

Say: "Every step I take is sacred."

Step over it slowly, visualizing yourself stepping into power.

Confidence & Power

I trust my voice

I move with purpose & ease.

I am capable of leading my own life.

I carry strength in my softness.

I embody quiet power.

I trust myself to rise.

I choose courage, not comfort.

I am the architect of my future.

My confidence is not conditional.

I am stronger than I've ever known.

Boundaries & Protection

Spell: The Black Stone Guard Ritual

Hold a black stone (obsidian, onyx, or a pebble).

Blow on it, imagining your stress or vulnerability transferring to it.

Say: "You guard me. I move freely."

Keep it in your pocket for the day or sleep with it under your pillow.

Boundaries & Protection

I choose what I allow in my life.

My peace is my responsibility.

I do not explain my boundaries.

Saying no is a full sentence.

I protect my energy with love.

I release what drains me.

I honor the space I need.

I choose relationships that nourish me.

I am not responsible for others' reactions.

I walk away from what hurts my spirit.

I trust the quiet voice inside me.

I listen to my gut.

My inner wisdom is sharp & clear.

I DON'T NEED OUTSIDE VALIDATION.

I KNOW WHAT'S BEST FOR ME.

I FOLLOW MY INNER COMPASS.

I AM IN TUNE WITH MY TRUTH.

I CHOOSE WHAT FEELS ALIGNED.

I TRUST WHAT I SENSE.

MY INTUITION IS A SACRED GUIDE.

Emotional Healing

Spell: The Burn & Breathe Ritual

Write your emotions on paper, no structure needed.

Burn it safely (or tear it & flush it).

As smoke or paper lifts, say: "It moved through me, not into me."

Emotional Healing

I AM ALLOWED TO FEEL EVERYTHING.

I HONOR MY GRIEF WITH GRACE.

MY EMOTIONS ARE NOT TOO MUCH.

I ALLOW MYSELF TO CRY & CLEANSE.

I GIVE MY PAIN A VOICE & LET IT MOVE.

I MEET MY WOUNDS WITH COMPASSION.

I DO NOT RUSH MY HEALING.

I FEEL DEEPLY & RISE GENTLY.

I LET GO OF GUILT I DO NOT OWN.

I AM SAFE TO FEEL.

I AM MY OWN SANCTUARY.

I TAKE CARE OF MYSELF WITH LOVE.

I PRIORITIZE WHAT BRINGS ME JOY.

I CHECK IN WITH MYSELF OFTEN.

I HONOR MY BOUNDARIES WITH DEVOTION.

I SAY YES TO MYSELF.

I REST BECAUSE I DESERVE IT.

I KEEP SACRED PROMISES TO MYSELF.

I SPEAK LOVINGLY TO MY SOUL.

I POUR INTO MYSELF WITHOUT APOLOGY.

Leadership & Influence

Spell: The Flame Claim Ritual

Light a candle & place your hand near the flame (not in it).

Say: "I lead with integrity. I burn with truth."

Let the candle burn as you speak a leadership-focused affirmation aloud.

Leadership & Influence

I lead by example.

I use my voice with intention.

I inspire through authenticity.

I take up space with grace.

I lead with heart & conviction.

I influence through presence.

I take responsibility for my power.

I model integrity.

I speak with clarity.

I embody my values.

Gratitude, Growth & Joy

Spell: The Fruit & Seed Blessing Ritual

Hold a piece of fruit or something sweet.

Whisper thanks for one thing in your life before each bite.

Say: "I receive joy with each taste."

OR

Hold a seed (any kind). Whisper to it:

"I plant growth. I water it with truth."

Bury it in soil or a pot, even if it never grows, it's symbolic.

Gratitude, Growth & Joy

I notice the good in each day.

I celebrate small victories.

I choose joy in ordinary moments.

I am grateful for my growth.

I give thanks for what's yet to come.

I find light even in the dark.

I delight in being alive.

I welcome joy into my body.

I see beauty in the simple.

I am grateful for this breath.

I learn from every moment.

I am allowed to make mistakes.

I am curious & open.

I GROW IN MY OWN TIME.

I TURN CHALLENGES INTO WISDOM.

I SEE CHANGE AS A GIFT.

I EXPAND BEYOND MY LIMITS.

I STRETCH INTO NEW TRUTHS.

I WELCOME DISCOMFORT AS A TEACHER.

I EVOLVE WITH GRACE.

Grounding, Clarity & Becoming

Spell: The Barefoot Grounding & Cloaking Ritual

Stand barefoot on earth (grass, sand, tile if needed).

Wrap yourself in a blanket or shawl.

Say: "I am becoming. I wear the truth I've grown into. I root into now."

Breathe deeply & imagine cords dropping from your feet into the earth.

Sit in silence, visualizing the version of you you're stepping into.

Grounding, Clarity & Becoming

I root myself in the present.

I make grounded choices.

I return to my breath.

I see clearly & choose wisely.

I ground into the moment.

I trust the now.

I anchor myself in truth.

I slow down to hear myself.

I pause with intention.

I find clarity in stillness.

I am already whole.

I am not who I was & that's beautiful.

I step into myself more each day.

I am not afraid to be seen.

I grow with intention.

I carry sacred fire.

I walk my talk.

I am becoming something sacred.

I choose who I become.

I am the embodiment of change.

A FAREWELL TO YOU

AFFIRMATIONS DIDN'T SOLVE ALL MY PROBLEMS, BUT THEY DID
SOMETHING JUST AS IMPORTANT.

THEY REMINDED ME I WAS ALLOWED TO QUESTION EVERYTHING.
TO IMAGINE MORE. TO GET CREATIVE WITH MY DREAMS.
TO CHOOSE A NEW THOUGHT, THEN ANOTHER, THEN ANOTHER.

IF YOU'VE MADE IT TO THE END OF THIS BOOK,
MAYBE YOU'VE STARTED ASKING DIFFERENT QUESTIONS.
MAYBE YOU'RE STARTING TO FEEL THE SHIFT.
KEEP GOING.

LET YOUR STORY UNRAVEL. LET IT RETHREAD ITSELF.
LET YOUR TRUTH BE FLUID, LIKE INK, LIKE WATER, LIKE BREATH.

WHEN YOU NEED TO, COME BACK TO THE BEGINNING.
WHISPER THE FIRST WORD AGAIN.

START OVER. START SOFTER. START STRONGER.

I AM BECAUSE I FEEL, I DO BECAUSE I LOVE.

I SPEAK INTO EXISTENCE, SO THAT I MAY SEE THE WORLD
UNFOLD BEFORE ME.

I AM THAT I FEEL & I FEEL THAT I AM,
SO THAT I KNOW, THAT I AM.

www.ingramcontent.com/pod-product-compliance
Lightning Source LLC
Chambersburg PA
CBHW070354130626
46556CB00007B/3162